How to... CLONE A SHEEP

How to...
CLONE A SHEEP

By HAZEL RICHARDSON

Illustrated by
Andy Cooke

OXFORD
UNIVERSITY PRESS

For Becky, Cathy and Sam for being great friends

OXFORD
UNIVERSITY PRESS

Great Clarendon Street, Oxford OX2 6DP

Oxford University Press is a department of the University of Oxford.
It furthers the University's objective of excellence in research, scholarship,
and education by publishing worldwide in

Oxford New York

Athens Auckland Bangkok Bogotá Buenos Aires Calcutta
Cape Town Chennai Dar es Salaam Delhi Florence Hong Kong Istanbul
Karachi Kuala Lumpur Madrid Melbourne Mexico City Mumbai
Nairobi Paris São Paulo Singapore Taipei Tokyo Toronto Warsaw

with associated companies in Berlin Ibadan

Oxford is a registered trade mark of Oxford University Press
in the UK and in certain other countries

British Library Cataloguing in Publication Data available

ISBN 0-19-910589-8

1 3 5 7 9 10 8 6 4 2

Printed and bound in Great Britain by
Cox & Wyman Ltd, Reading, Berkshire

Contents

HOW TO CLONE A SHEEP

On 5 July 1996, something happened that would change the course of human history. This was more amazing than people landing on the Moon. The news spread around the world within hours. Some people were delighted and excited. Other people were horrified. Some people even said that we were now as powerful as God!

What had happened?

A lamb had been born in a shed in Scotland.

It might seem silly that the birth of a lamb could make millions of people excited or scared, but this was a very special lamb. It was called Dolly and it was an exact copy, or clone, of another sheep. It was the first time that scientists had successfully cloned an adult animal, and it means that soon we may be able to clone any other animal, or even a human ifwe want to!

In this book, you will learn all about:

- ◎ what DNA and genes are
- ◎ how embryos grow into animals
- ◎ what cloning is
- ◎ why it is so difficult to do
- ◎ why we will be able to clone humans if we want to
- ◎ why cloning scares some people
- ◎ the scientists who discovered how to clone animals
- ◎ how you can clone plants and an animal at home

CHAPTER ONE

WHAT IS A CLONE?

A clone is an exact copy of a living thing. Scientists have been able to clone plants and bacteria (germs) for a long time. Now Dolly has been born, we can clone adult animals and probably even humans as well!

Making a copy of a living thing is much more difficult than making a copy of something that isn't living, like a mountain bike. For many years, people have tried to make robots that look and behave like humans. In science fiction films and TV shows, there are often androids – robots that are part human and part robot. But in real life, scientists haven't been very successful. Robots still look like hunks of metal. They don't move like we do, and they don't think like we do.

Robots don't *look* like living things because they are built out of materials that are not living. Living things are built out of tiny building blocks called cells. Scientists can't make their own cells yet.

Robots don't *behave* like living things because robots and computers are programmed (given instructions about how to behave) Computer programs are very complicated, but not a millionth as complicated as what living things are programmed by – DNA.

But I'm not programmed like a computer!

Yes, you are!
Everything about you
depends on the instructions
you get from DNA. This means that if we could copy your DNA, we could make another human that looks just like you! This human would be your clone.

DNA ....

- ◎   DNA is a very complicated chemical called deoxyribonucleic acid. Scientists use the initials DNA so that they don't have to write its name out in full all the time.

- ◎   It looks like a long, twisty ladder and it carries a secret code that the body can read. This code tells living things what they should look like, what they should eat, and how they should grow.

- ◎   Everything about how you look depends on what the code in DNA says.

There are millions of copies of the DNA code inside you. You can go and find them if you shrink to a tiny size and go inside your body!

The Incredible Journey

There are things going on inside your body that you wouldn't believe. Inside you are motorways, factories and even an army that kills invaders!

Here you are on the arm. It looks like a forest with tall hair trees towering above you. Go and look in a pore — it looks like a deep well stretching down as far as you can see. What happens if I push you in?

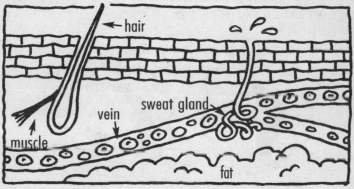

Now you're under your skin, you can see how much is going on. Here's a sweat gland, squirting out liquid. Here's a muscle, pulling the hair up when you get cold. And here's what looks like a road, full of red liquid. This is your blood. If you shrink even more, you can go for a ride in it!

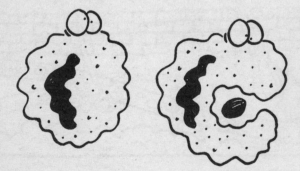

You can't usually see these tiny things in your blood. They are red blood cells. They're round and have a dent in the middle, and they are used to carry oxygen from your lungs to the rest of your body. You're now small enough to sit in the dent, but hang on — it's a bumpy ride!

As you ride along, you notice other cells. These are white blood cells. They move along by stretching bits of themselves out and pulling the rest along. They are a dedicated army of cells that seek out and eat any germs that get inside you.

White blood cells have a dark blob inside them. As you rush along the blood road, you see that the sides of the road are made of block-like cells. These also have dark blobs inside them. In fact, every cell you see has a dark blob — apart from the red blood cells.

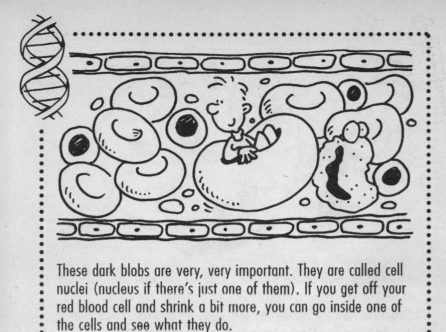

These dark blobs are very, very important. They are called cell nuclei (nucleus if there's just one of them). If you get off your red blood cell and shrink a bit more, you can go inside one of the cells and see what they do.

nucleus

Here you are inside a cell. It's just like a factory. There's a conveyor belt putting things together. And the weird sausage-shaped blobs are little power stations.

nucleus

Here's a close-up of the nucleus. Inside it are what look like lots of very long, coiled up pieces of string. These are called chromosomes. Chromosomes are made up of DNA. Every cell in your body has these chromosomes, except red blood cells. Red blood cells need extra space inside them to carry oxygen around your body.

What has DNA and what doesn't?..........

Every living thing on Earth has some DNA inside it. Simple living things like bacteria can carry all their DNA on only one chromosome. They have only a small amount of DNA because they don't need many instructions about how to grow. More complicated animals and plants have lots of chromosomes. Humans have 46 chromosomes in most cells in their bodies. You need this much DNA because there are so many different parts of you that need instructions: your hair and eye colour; how to grow bones, your heart, your liver and all your other organs; how to move – everything!

14

Here's what human chromosomes look like.

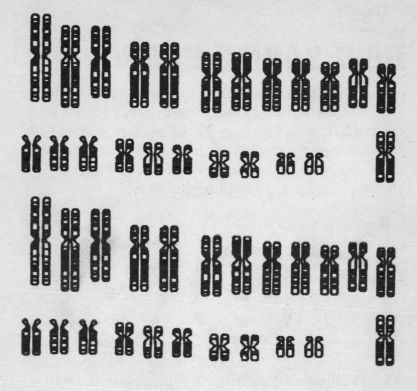

Do you notice something strange? It looks like there are two copies of each chromosome. But why would we need two copies?

We have two copies of the DNA instructions because we get one set from our mother and one set from our father.

CHAPTER TWO

HOW BABIES GROW

All animals, including humans, reproduce by joining a cell from the father, called a sperm cell, to a cell from the mother, called an egg. These are very special cells because they are made with just one copy of the DNA code – only 23 chromosomes. When the egg and sperm cell join, it is called fertilization.

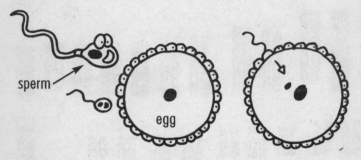

The 23 chromosomes from the sperm join the 23 chromosomes from the egg to make 46 chromosomes. Once the egg cell has all 46 chromsomes, it has all the instructions it needs to develop into a new human being, so it gets growing!

An unfertilised egg is tiny and round. For a human egg to become a new human being, it needs to grow arms, legs, a head – everything. This takes a long time. To begin with, the cell splits into two, and into two again until it is a ball of cells. Then something amazing happens. The cells read their DNA code and each one takes on a job to do in the new body.

Once the cells have taken on the jobs they're going to do, they look at the bits of DNA inside them that tell them how to do that job. Then they become the kind of cell that they are going to be in the new body. The ball of cells starts to grow arms, legs, a heart, lungs, kidneys and all the other bits that you have. This developing ball of cells is called an embryo.

It takes about ten weeks for the egg to grow into an embryo that looks like a human baby. But it is very tiny. It has to grow inside the mother for another seven months or so before it can face life outside on its own.

Before we knew all this, people used to have some funny ideas about how babies were made.

Fertilization Facts
Part 1

Ancient Greece, around 350 BC.

This is Aristotle, one of the most important scientists ever. People at this time are beginning to ask questions about why animals, plants and humans look like they do. Aristotle has written lots of books about this that will still be used thousands of years later.

Today, he's trying to work out how babies are made. He's busy breaking open hens' eggs and looking at the baby chicks inside. This seems like a cruel thing to do, but it is the only way he can find out how babies grow.

He notices that at first, the unborn chick just looks like a tiny blob. It grows its head, legs and wings before it hatches. He thinks that a tiny part of the egg can grow into a whole new animal!

Aristotle is right, but not everyone agrees with him. Most men like to think that women just give the baby food to grow and that the baby is made by the man. A Roman called Seneca says that every sperm has a tiny human inside it. It is so tiny that it can't be seen, but all it has to do is grow bigger once it has food from the mother. He says that it doesn't need to make arms, legs and a head — they're already there.

Who was right?

Be A Genetic Scientist:
WATCH AN EMBYRO GROWING!

You can't watch a chicken embryo growing like Aristotle did because it's too difficult to get eggs that grow chicks inside them. Eggs that you can buy in the shop are unfertilized and would never turn into chickens. But you can watch an embryo growing very easily if you collect some frog spawn!

WHAT YOU'LL NEED
◎ some frog spawn from a pond
(you'll only find this in the spring. It's a jelly-like mess full of little black dots)

◎ a net

◎ some jam jars of pond water

WHAT TO DO
1   In early spring, find a pond with frog spawn. (A science teacher at school should be able to help you.) The frog spawn is frog eggs that have been fertilised. If you look closely at them, you will see that the eggs are round and whitish clear, with a black dot in the middle. This is the nucleus, which contains DNA for building the frog.

2   Collect some frog spawn using the net, then put the spawn into a jam jar of the pond water and take it home.

3   Keep the frog spawn in a safe place and watch what happens to them. They don't need any food, just water.

You will be able to see the frog eggs splitting up and growing into tadpoles.

Please be kind to animals. When you have grown your tadpoles, take them back to the pond so that they can grow into frogs. Once the eggs have become tadpoles, they need food from the pond or they will die.

Spying on cells..

After the microscope was invented in 1609, scientists were able to see cells and the nucleus inside them. They watched egg cells splitting into two new cells and growing. But they still believed in Seneca's idea about how animals are made. The first scientists who looked at sperm drew them with a little man inside each one. They were sure they could see them!

By the end of the 19th century, scientists had finally realised that a single egg cell grows into a completely new animal made up of millions of cells. This made them very puzzled.

The only answer people could think of was...

It sounded sensible. After all, polar bears were white and they all lived in the same place. Grizzly bears were all brown and they lived in the same place. So animals and plants must look like they do just because of where they live.

It was sensible but wrong. When polar bears in a zoo have babies, they are still white – even though they no longer need to be camouflaged against the ice. A grizzly bear made to live in the snow doesn't have white babies. There was something in animals and plants that told their children to look just like them. What could it be?

Then Charles Darwin came along.

22

Fertilization Facts
Part II
England, 1859

Leave this to me!

Charles Darwin shot to fame in 1859, when he published one of the most famous books ever written. It was called *On the Origin of Species* and it caused a lot of trouble! Before Darwin came along, most people believed in the Bible story of creation, where God had made every animal and plant on Earth. But Darwin and some other scientists discovered something very strange. They found fossils of animals, like dinosaurs, that were no longer alive. They also noticed that some of these extinct animals looked like animals that *were* still alive. Darwin decided that animals could change from one type of animal into another type over thousands or millions of years. He called this process evolution.

What people found hardest to believe about Darwin's idea of evolution was that humans had evolved from apes! They were shocked and horrified at the thought. Religious people laughed at him.

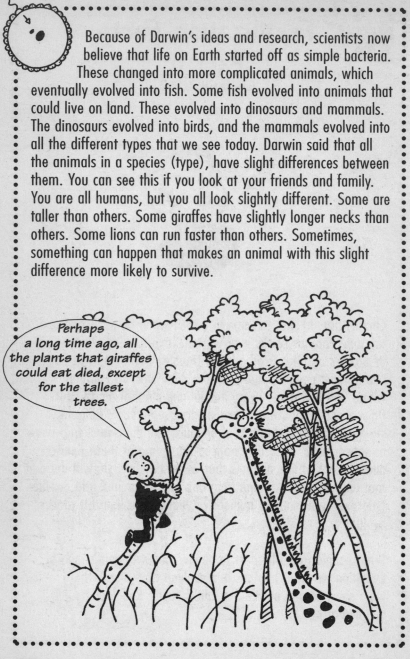

Because of Darwin's ideas and research, scientists now believe that life on Earth started off as simple bacteria. These changed into more complicated animals, which eventually evolved into fish. Some fish evolved into animals that could live on land. These evolved into dinosaurs and mammals. The dinosaurs evolved into birds, and the mammals evolved into all the different types that we see today. Darwin said that all the animals in a species (type), have slight differences between them. You can see this if you look at your friends and family. You are all humans, but you all look slightly different. Some are taller than others. Some giraffes have slightly longer necks than others. Some lions can run faster than others. Sometimes, something can happen that makes an animal with this slight difference more likely to survive.

Perhaps a long time ago, all the plants that giraffes could eat died, except for the tallest trees.

The giraffes with longer necks are more likely to survive, because they can reach higher branches to eat the leaves.

The longer-necked giraffes have babies, which also have longer necks. Soon, all giraffes will have longer necks than they used to — the giraffes have evolved!

But even though Darwin could work out that animals could change, he couldn't work out why the children of long-necked giraffes also had long necks.

Babies look like their parents because the blood from the mother gets mixed up with the blood from the father!

Wrong again!

Keeping it in the family.......................

Darwin's cousin, Francis Galton, thought that this was a load of nonsense. He did an experiment on rabbits to prove Darwin wrong. (What a nice relative to have!) He took a white female rabbit and mated her with a white male rabbit. Then he took some blood from a black rabbit and injected it into the white female rabbit. Next, he waited for the white rabbit's babies to be born, to see what colour they were.

Were the babies:
   A. white?
   B. black?

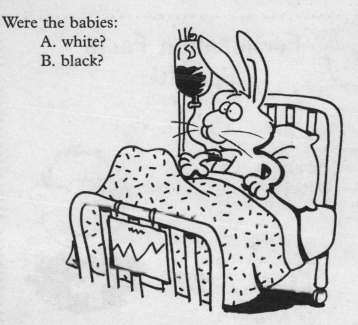

The baby rabbits were all white, even though their mother had been injected with black rabbit blood.

So, Galton knew that how you look has nothing to do with your mum and dad's blood. The reason why we look like our parents remained a mystery.

CHAPTER THREE

GENIUS GENES

It was a pity that Darwin didn't get to meet a monk called Gregor Mendel. He discovered why babies look like their parents at the same time as Darwin was asking his questions.

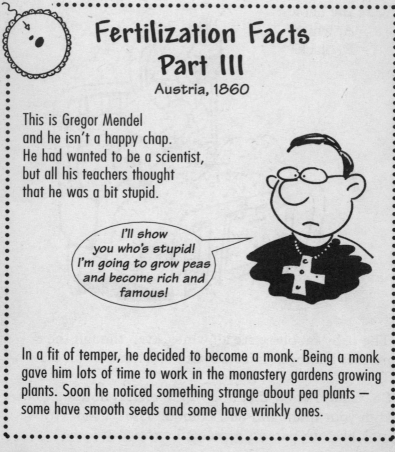

Fertilization Facts Part III
Austria, 1860

This is Gregor Mendel and he isn't a happy chap. He had wanted to be a scientist, but all his teachers thought that he was a bit stupid.

I'll show you who's stupid! I'm going to grow peas and become rich and famous!

In a fit of temper, he decided to become a monk. Being a monk gave him lots of time to work in the monastery gardens growing plants. Soon he noticed something strange about pea plants — some have smooth seeds and some have wrinkly ones.

Peas are the seeds of pea plants. When a pea is planted, it grows into a new pea plant. Just like animals, baby plants are made from a special female egg cell and a special male pollen cell. If you look at a flower, you can find these special cells.

Most flowers look like this…

This piece in the middle of the flower is called the style. The egg cell is hidden deep inside it. If you touch the top of the style, you will feel that it is sticky.

These long things are called stamens. The fine powder on them is pollen.

The petals are usually bright and colourful and are used to attract insects. Plants can't move like humans and so they need help to get the pollen to the egg cell.

Usually, insects pick up some pollen when they come to a flower. They fly to another flower and some of the pollen gets stuck onto the sticky style. The pollen cells dig a tunnel down through it to get to the egg.

Scientists can make flowers have babies by taking some of the pollen from one flower and placing it on the style of another flower. This is called crossing. Mendel realized that he could cross a wrinkly pea plant with a smooth pea plant to see what kind of peas the baby pea plants would make. He found that all the baby plants made smooth peas. What had happened to the wrinkliness?

Mendel was very curious and decided to see what happened when these smooth pea baby plants had baby plants of their own. Some of these plants made wrinkly peas — the wrinkliness had come back! What on earth was going on?

Mendel came up with an explanation. He said that each pea plant has instructions inside it, telling it which kind of pea to make. He called these instructions factors. Today, we call them genes. Each pea plant gets two gene instructions about which kind of pea to make — one from its mother and one from its father plant.

Make smooth peas!

Make wrinkly peas!

The smooth pea gene is dominant. The wrinkly pea gene is weaker, or recessive.

I'm the strongest!

Errrgh!

So if a smooth gene and a smooth gene join together, the pea plant will have smooth seeds; if a smooth gene and a wrinkly gene join together, the plant will still have smooth seeds. But if two wrinkly genes join together, the pea plant will have wrinkly seeds.

You can see on the chart below how this explains Mendel's results.

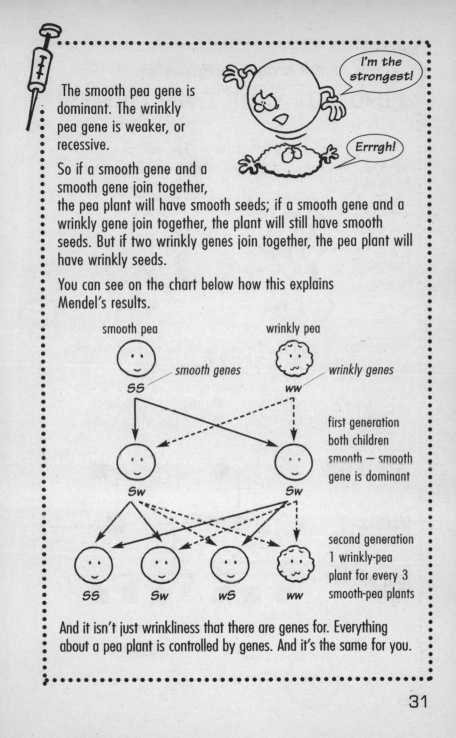

smooth pea

wrinkly pea

smooth genes

wrinkly genes

SS

ww

first generation both children smooth — smooth gene is dominant

Sw

Sw

second generation 1 wrinkly-pea plant for every 3 smooth-pea plants

SS   Sw   wS   ww

And it isn't just wrinkliness that there are genes for. Everything about a pea plant is controlled by genes. And it's the same for you.

Be A Genetic Scientist:
FIND OUT YOUR OWN GENES!

There are genes for all kinds of things. For instance, did you know that there is a gene for whether or not your ear has a lobe?

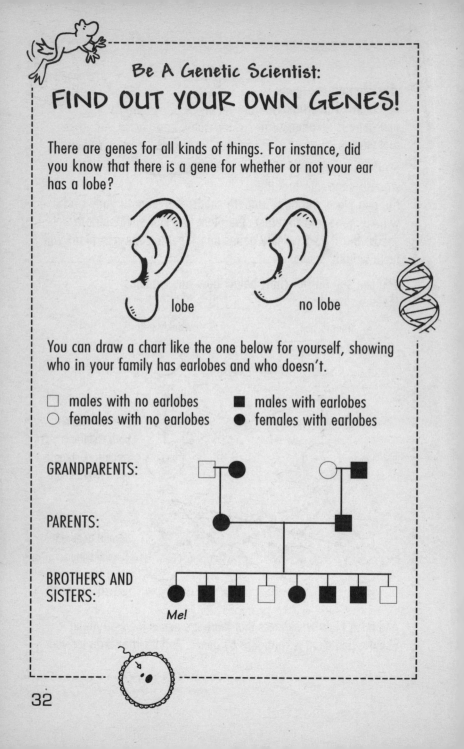

lobe   no lobe

You can draw a chart like the one below for yourself, showing who in your family has earlobes and who doesn't.

☐ males with no earlobes   ■ males with earlobes
○ females with no earlobes   ● females with earlobes

GRANDPARENTS:

PARENTS:

BROTHERS AND SISTERS:

Me!

How do I get these genes from my parents?.............................

Remember the chromosomes inside you? There are
two copies of each one. One of the copies comes from
your father and one comes from your mother. Each
chromosome carries the genes for different things
about you. Because there are two copies, the cells
have to decide which gene they are going to listen to.
Sometimes they listen to both and then you look like a
mix of the two genes.

The joining of two recessive genes is what happened
in Mendel's wrinkly pea plants.

Unfortunately, when Mendel tried to tell other scientists about his pea plants, everyone ignored him.

Mendel soon gave up and started working on apples instead. He got into a bitter argument with the government about his taxes, had heart disease, and smoked 20 cigars a day. He spent his last days sitting on a couch with his feet in bandages, suffering from dropsy. (Dropsy is a horrible disease that makes you swell up.) He died in 1884, a very unhappy and bitter man.

Mendel's work was discovered 16 years after his death, by three scientists who were squabbling about who discovered dominant and recessive genes first. It turned out that Mendel had beaten them all to it!

CHAPTER FOUR

THE LINK BETWEEN GENES AND DNA

So, by 1900 we knew that it was genes that make us look the way we do. But scientists didn't know where these genes were. What were they made of?

We now know that genes are made of DNA, which is in long strings called chromosomes. But this was discovered completely by accident…

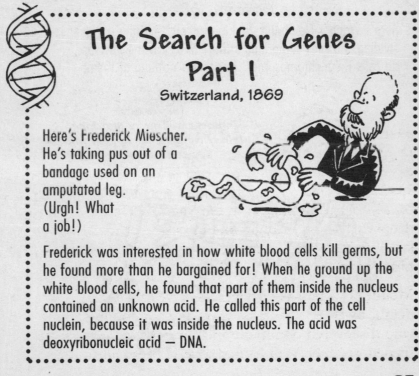

The Search for Genes Part I
Switzerland, 1869

Here's Frederick Miescher. He's taking pus out of a bandage used on an amputated leg. (Urgh! What a job!)

Frederick was interested in how white blood cells kill germs, but he found more than he bargained for! When he ground up the white blood cells, he found that part of them inside the nucleus contained an unknown acid. He called this part of the cell nuclein, because it was inside the nucleus. The acid was deoxyribonucleic acid — DNA.

DNA – a marvellous mystery.................

Frederick had no idea what DNA was for. At that time, nobody had seen chromosomes inside cells, and nobody knew about Mendel's amazing discoveries of how babies could look like their parents. Frederick carried on working with DNA though, and discovered a very important clue: sperm were made up of this DNA and very little else. Could this show a link between how babies looked and DNA?

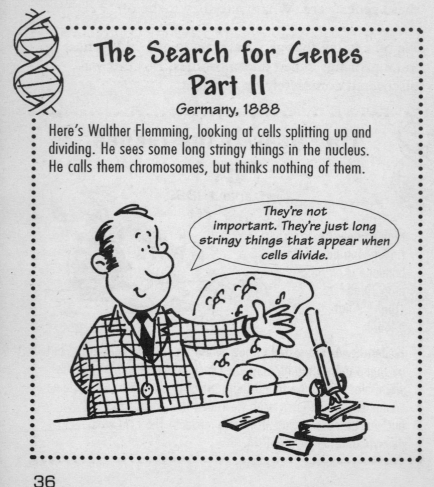

The Search for Genes Part II
Germany, 1888

Here's Walther Flemming, looking at cells splitting up and dividing. He sees some long stringy things in the nucleus. He calls them chromosomes, but thinks nothing of them.

They're not important. They're just long stringy things that appear when cells divide.

Chromosome contents ....

The link between genes and chromosomes was only noticed in 1907, by Thomas Hunt Morgan. He wasn't convinced by all this new-fangled Mendel gene stuff. He decided to breed fruit flies to see if Mendel's ideas about genes were true. They were! He found that the only part of the cell that could contain the genes had to be a long stringy thing – a chromosome.

The problem now was that chromosomes are not just made up of DNA. They have a coating of protein all round them. Scientists were puzzled. What carried the gene instructions – the protein or the DNA? Then, an important experiment with some nasty germs gave us the answer...

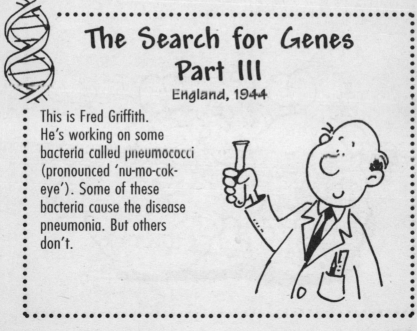

The Search for Genes
Part III
England, 1944

This is Fred Griffith. He's working on some bacteria called pneumococci (pronounced 'nu-mo-cok-eye'). Some of these bacteria cause the disease pneumonia. But others don't.

Bacteria don't have babies like animals and plants. When they want to make more of themselves, they get thinner in the middle and split into two. This makes two new bacteria, each of which is exactly like the parent bacteria. Because the two new bacteria are identical, they are clones!

Be a Genetic Scientist:
CLONE YOUR OWN BACTERIA!

You can see how a bacteria splits up and makes copies of itself in an experiment using jelly.

WHAT YOU'LL NEED
- ◎ some jelly mix cubes
- ◎ two old yoghurt pots
- ◎ a toothpick (a plastic one is best)
- ◎ sterilizing solution (like Dettol or Milton)
- ◎ clingfilm

WHAT TO DO
1. Sterilize one of the yoghurt pots by leaving it to soak in the sterilizing liquid.
2. Make up a small amount of jelly, then pour it into the yoghurt pot — not right to the top. Cover it immediately with the clingfilm.
3. When the jelly has set, peel back a little bit of the clingfilm. Quickly rub one finger around your gums and teeth and then press it against the jelly.
4. Cover the pot up again and leave it in a warm place (where no one will find it and throw it out!).
5. Check the jelly every day to see what is growing on it. Soon, you will see little blobs on the jelly. These are bacteria from your mouth. You can clone these.

Urgh! It's going all furry!

6   Sterilize the other yoghurt pot.
7   Make up more jelly, pour it into the pot to set and cover it with clingfilm just like you did before. (Make sure there is an air space between the jelly and the clingfilm.)
8   Sterilize the toothpick.
9   Carefully open the pot that has bacteria in and just touch the toothpick into a lump of bacteria. This should pick up a few bacteria. Touch the toothpick onto the new jelly and cover it up.
10 Leave it in a safe warm place and see what happens.

BE CAREFUL
Bacteria cause diseases and can be dangerous!
Throw away the cartons and the jelly when you finish this experiment.
ALWAYS wash your hands after you've touched the experiment.

WHAT HAPPENS?
The few bacteria that you pick up on the toothpick divide up many times to make many more bacteria. These are all clones of the bacteria you had in your mouth. (Yuck! Now you know why you should clean your teeth.)

The Search for Genes
Part IV
Back again to England, 1944

Fred Griffiths found that the bacteria that caused pneumonia always made new bacteria that caused pneumonia. Bacteria that didn't cause the disease always made new bacteria that didn't cause the disease. So, Fred knew that causing a disease is something that the bacteria inherit — just like you inherit eye colour from your parents.

Fred wanted to know which bit of the bacteria carried the disease-causing genes. So he did a really nasty experiment on some rabbits. He killed some disease bacteria by heating them up. Then he injected them into a rabbit. The rabbit didn't get ill.

Hurry up and bring me some more carrots!

Then Fred mixed up the dead bacteria with some friendly bacteria. When he injected the mixture, the rabbits got sick. The friendly bacteria were following instructions from the dead nasty bacteria. All Fred had to do was to find out which bit of the dead bacteria carried the instructions. He broke open the bacteria, separated them into all their bits, and tried the experiment again and again until he found the only bit of the dead bacteria that made the friendly bacteria turn nasty. And this bit was the chromosome.

Finally finding genes..............................

Fred was convinced that the genes were carried on the DNA part of the chromosome, but he couldn't prove it. Other scientists thought that the protein coating on the chromosomes carried the genes instead. It was left to Oswald Avery to save the day...

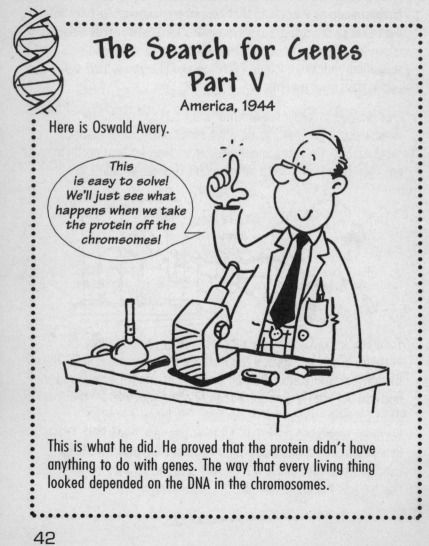

The Search for Genes Part V
America, 1944

Here is Oswald Avery.

This is easy to solve! We'll just see what happens when we take the protein off the chromsomes!

This is what he did. He proved that the protein didn't have anything to do with genes. The way that every living thing looked depended on the DNA in the chromosomes.

CHAPTER FIVE

CRACKING THE CODE

Now scientists knew that the genes were carried on chromosomes made of DNA, the race was on to find out how the cells could read the genes. Genes work by telling the cells which proteins to make. You've probably heard of protein to do with food, but believe it or not, there are hundreds of types of protein – including the type of proteins that your body makes, which make you look the way you do.

Here are some important proteins made by cells inside your body:

◎ muscle protein

◎ haemoglobin in red blood cells, which carries oxygen around your body

◎ enzymes, which break down food inside you

◎ keratin, which makes hair and nails

◎ collagen, which makes your skin stretchy

But how can a long stringy piece of DNA tell a stomach cell to make a protein that digests food? To find this out, scientists had to see how DNA was put together. The first scientist to find this out would know exactly how genes worked and would be rich and famous.

The DNA Race

Here we are in the 1950s ready for this exciting race to see which scientist can be the first to work out what DNA looks like. The winner will receive a lovely Nobel Prize and lots of money. Let's have a look at the runners.

Linus Pauling — surely the favourite man to win the race. Has already won the Nobel Prize and has worked out what proteins look like. They are a twisty spiral shape called a helix.

Rosalind Franklin — a clever woman who knows how to take X-ray pictures of DNA, which should help her. But she might be slowed down because she's one of the few women in a university dominated by men.

45

And they're off!

Linus Pauling goes straight into the lead by saying that DNA is a helix, just like some proteins. But he falls at the first hurdle when he says that DNA has three strands twisted round each other. (It actually has two.) Bad luck!

So, there are four runners in the race now. Maurice Wilkins is in the lead slightly, because he knows how to take pictures of DNA. He joins up with Rosalind Franklin, who can also take pictures of DNA. Maurice and Rosalind pull further into the lead.

They are closely followed by James Watson and Francis Crick. But they're not really getting anywhere because they do most of their research by sitting in a pub and trying to build little models out of wire.

But, what's this? Maurice and Rosalind have fallen out! Rosalind is starting to work on her own, and she's doing very well. She's pulling ahead of Maurice. Maurice is annoyed. He's slowing down to talk to Watson and Crick.

Maurice shows Watson and Crick a picture that Rosalind took – without asking her! Is this allowed? It must be, because Maurice hasn't been disqualified.

But, what's this? Another surprise – two people have run on to the race track: Erwin Chargaff and Jerry Donahue. They're talking to Watson and Crick, telling them how the two strands of DNA join together.

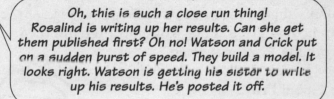

Oh, this is such a close run thing! Rosalind is writing up her results. Can she get them published first? Oh no! Watson and Crick put on a sudden burst of speed. They build a model. It looks right. Watson is getting his sister to write up his results. He's posted it off.

> *Watson and Crick win the race! Rosalind limps home in second place, closely followed by Maurice Wilkins in third.*

Looking inside DNA.................................

James Watson and Francis Crick later won the Nobel Prize for discovering the structure of DNA. Maurice Wilkins shared the prize with them because of the help he had given. Poor Rosalind Franklin died before the Prize was given.
Dead people can't be awarded the Nobel Prize.

The model that Watson and Crick thought up looked like this. →

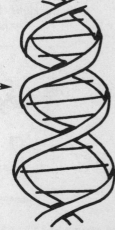

DNA looks like a twisty ladder. There are two sides, with rungs joining them together. This is called a double helix.
Believe it or not, those rungs carry all the genes you need to

48

make you look exactly like you. This is how it works. There are four special molecules, called bases, in DNA. The rungs are made up of two bases joined together in the middle. The four bases are called:

- ○ adenine
- ○ thymine
- ○ cytosine
- ○ guanine

To make things easier scientists just call them A, T, C and G.

A always joins to T to make up a rung. C always joins up to G to make a rung. So, a little bit of DNA could look like this.

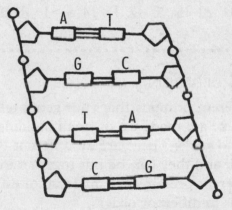

These four bases are very important because they make up a code.

Powerful proteins

All the different proteins that your genes tell your body to make are made up of small building blocks called amino acids. There are 20 different types of amino acid, and they can be put together into any order. Different proteins are made up of different amino acids in different orders.

amino acids

The DNA in all your cells has instructions about every protein that your body will ever need to make. But because different cells only need to make proteins for their own job (like stomach cells only need to make proteins that help them digest food) they only need to read part of the code – the bit that codes for that particular protein. The DNA has markers that show the cell where each bit of coding for the different proteins starts and finishes. When a cell wants to make a new protein, it finds the start marker for that protein and makes a copy of the protein's DNA code. This can then be sent out of the nucleus and given to the protein-making factories in the cell, which are called ribosomes. The job of making the DNA copy is done by a special worker called RNA polymerase. Here, we'll call her Poly for short.

How does the cell read the DNA code?...

Poly goes to the bit of the DNA that codes for the protein that needs to be made. She takes out a large pair of scissors and cuts the rungs in half so that she can pull the ladder apart a bit. Then Poly gets inside the ladder and wanders along the letters.

snip

snip

As she comes to each letter, she notes down what it is and then sends out for a copy of the letter that will join to it. Remember, A always joins to T and C always joins to G. So if she comes across a letter T, she asks for a letter A. If she finds a letter C, she asks for a letter G. Poly strings the letters together as she goes along.

This string of letters is called messenger RNA, or mRNA for short. This mRNA is a copy of the protein code on the DNA.

When Poly has finished copying all the letters in the bit of DNA for that protein, the DNA joins up again. The mRNA copy is sent out of the nucleus to the protein-making factory.

The DNA code that Poly has to copy can be thousands and thousands of letters long. Sometimes she makes a mistake.

When she does, the code is wrong, and when the mRNA is sent to the protein-making factory, the code cannot be read properly. This can mean that the protein is not made properly and doesn't work. This is called mutation.

Be A Genetic Scientist:
SEE HOW DNA CAN BE COPIED!

You can see how copying DNA works by making your own model of DNA out of pipe cleaners and plasticine.

WHAT YOU'LL NEED
◎ pipe cleaners
◎ four colours of plasticine — red, yellow, blue and green.

WHAT TO DO

1   Lay out two pipe cleaners side by side. These are the sides of the DNA ladder. You don't have to twist them around for this experiment.

2   Twist other pipe cleaners around them for the rungs, like this.

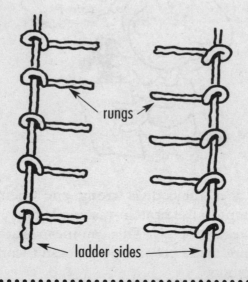

rungs

ladder sides

3   Make up a code for your DNA. This can be something like: TTACGT.
   ● For every letter T, put a blue blob on one side of your DNA chain.
   ● For every letter A, put a green blob.
   ● For every letter C, put a yellow blob.
   ● For every letter G, put a red blob.
   Great! One side of your DNA is ready.

4   Remember that A always joins to T, and C always joins to G. So, on the other side…

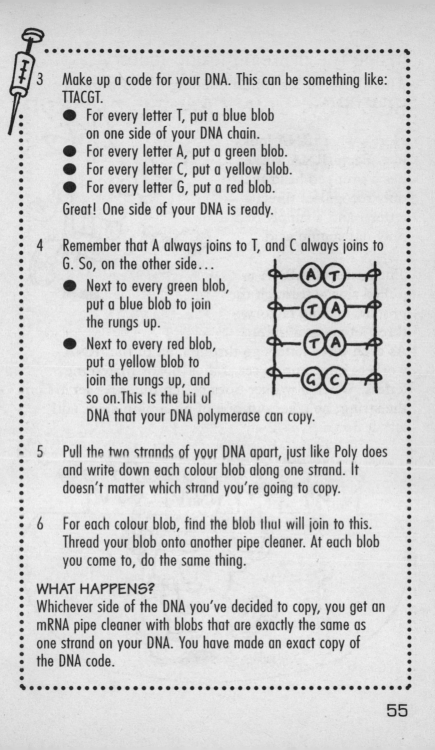

   ● Next to every green blob, put a blue blob to join the rungs up.
   ● Next to every red blob, put a yellow blob to join the rungs up, and so on. This is the bit of DNA that your DNA polymerase can copy.

5   Pull the two strands of your DNA apart, just like Poly does and write down each colour blob along one strand. It doesn't matter which strand you're going to copy.

6   For each colour blob, find the blob that will join to this. Thread your blob onto another pipe cleaner. At each blob you come to, do the same thing.

WHAT HAPPENS?
Whichever side of the DNA you've decided to copy, you get an mRNA pipe cleaner with blobs that are exactly the same as one strand on your DNA. You have made an exact copy of the DNA code.

Inside the protein-making factory...........

The ribosome is a round building full of workers called tRNA.

Here's what tRNA looks like. Each tRNA worker has a pronged head that only recognises three letters, and a supply of only one amino acid.

The string of mRNA is pulled slowly through the protein-making factory, three letters at a time.

As each three letters go through, all of the tRNA workers queue up to see if their heads match the letters. When a worker does match the three letters on the string, he takes out one of his amino acids and lays it down.

mRNA

ribosome

When a match has been made, the string continues to be pulled through the factory until the next three letters are lined up. The workers try and match themselves up again. The worker that matches the code lays down his amino acid and joins it to the first one.

After thousands of amino acids are joined together, a protein is made.

So now you know how a DNA code works!

CHAPTER SIX

TO CLONE OR NOT TO CLONE...?

Every cell has a complete copy of the DNA code that tells an animal everything it needs to build its body.

So in theory, you should be able to take any cell from an animal and let it grow into a new animal, like an embryo does. But cloning animals is in fact much more difficult than this.

Problems with cloning animals ....

As you've already seen, cloning bacteria isn't difficult.
It isn't difficult to clone plants either, as we'll see
later. But it *is* difficult to clone animals. This is
because there is a difference between the DNA in
animals and the DNA in plants.

In animals, something strange happens when the
embryo starts to grow. Cells that started off by looking
the same as each other take on different jobs.

All these cells look very different from each other. And not every cell needs to be able to make every

protein that the DNA codes for. For instance, when a cell becomes a stomach cell, it doesn't need to make the protein that gives you blue eyes. When a cell becomes a hair cell, it doesn't need to make muscle protein. Not only would it be a waste of energy, but it would make you look very weird!

On top of this, once a cell takes on a job in the body, it can't change into a different type of cell.

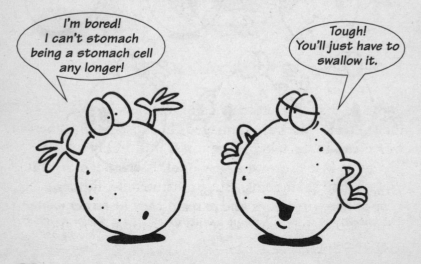

So the DNA a cell doesn't use is shut down. Each cell only uses about 10 per cent of the DNA code. This is why it's difficult to clone an adult animal. You can't just take any cell from an animal and grow it into a new animal, because some of the DNA won't be working. All the genes needed to make every cell in the new animal's body will be there, but not all of them are switched on.

Some very simple animals can grow new bits of themselves if they are damaged. For instance, a slow-worm can make its tail drop off if it is grabbed by a predator. It just grows a new one! Starfish can do this as well with their arms. But unfortunately, humans cannot grow new legs and arms if they lose them, because the cells have taken on individual jobs and cannot change.

In plant cells, the DNA is different. In plants, a cell can switch its DNA back on and become a different type of cell if it wants to. This means that you can take a cell from any bit of a plant and grow it into a completely new plant. This new plant is a clone!

Be A Genetic Scientist:
CLONE A PLANT!

Cloning plants is easy. You may have done it before without even realizing it.

WHAT YOU'LL NEED
- a plant — Busy Lizzies are ideal
- some plant pots and compost
- rooting hormone powder — you can buy this in garden centres or DIY stores
- a milk bottle
- water
- a pair of scissors

WHAT TO DO
1 Pick a side stem growing off your plant and cut it near to the main stem.

2 Dip the stem in the rooting powder.

3   Fill the milk bottle with water and put the stem in it. Leave it for a while and you should soon see roots growing.

4   Now plant it in a small plant pot of compost.

5   Keep the stem well watered. (Don't swamp it!)

6   The stem will grow into a new plant with exactly the same DNA as the first plant. You've grown a clone!

Trickier and trickier – cloning mammals

You can clone plants, bacteria and even frogs! But mammals are the hardest animals of all to clone because their babies grow inside the mother's body. It's all to do with giving the embryo food.

◎ A plant embryo has a food supply in the seed, which keeps it going until it germinates and grows into a plant.

◎ The embryos of amphibian animals like frogs have a food supply in their eggs.

◎ Mammals get their food from their mother, which is why babies have to grow inside their mother's womb (uterus) before they are born.

It would be much easier to just lay an egg.

The embryos in mammals make a special organ called the placenta, which attaches to the wall of the mother's uterus. The other end is joined to the embryo's stomach through a cord called the umbilical cord. This is how food travels from the mother to the embryo. (When you are born, a doctor cuts the cord off. This is what makes your belly button.)

Although cloning animals is very difficult, it could prove to be very useful. Here are some of the things the technique could be used for in the future:

- ○ making medicines
- ○ saving extinct species
- ○ growing organs for transplants

MAKING MEDICINES

There are some diseases caused when our bodies don't make a protein that they should.

In haemophilia, for example, the proteins that make blood clot are not coded properly by the person's DNA. If the haemophiliac is injured, they can bleed for a very long time – and may even die.

In diseases like this, scientists could make a copy of the gene for these proteins from someone who has DNA that *can* make them. If they put the copied gene into an animal like a cow, the cow will make the protein in its milk. These cows can then be cloned to make a herd of medicine-making cows.

SAVING EXTINCT SPECIES

Some species of wild animal are close to extinction (dying out completely). Scientists are using cloning at the moment to try to reproduce the giant panda, to stop the world losing them forever. If it works, hundreds or thousands of cloned pandas could be made.

GROWING ORGANS FOR TRANSPLANTS

Sometimes organs like kidneys, lungs, hearts and livers can stop working properly because of an illness.

An organ from a person who has died can sometimes be transplanted into someone with organ failure. But finding replacement organs is very difficult. For a start, the organ from the dead donor needs to be undamaged. And then the transplant has to be performed very quickly.

Even when the transplant is done there are problems. White blood cells go around your body destroying invaders and infections. They can recognize anything that doesn't belong to your body – including someone else's liver or kidney! The white blood cells will attack the donated organ.

The only way the white blood cells can be prevented from attacking the transplanted organ is by taking drugs that stop the white blood cells working. If they don't work properly, they can't hunt down *any* bacteria that get into your body, and so you can get ill very easily.

However, soon scientists might be able to take a cell out of your body and clone it to make any new organ they want. And because it would be a copy of your own liver or kidney, it wouldn't be attacked by your white blood cells.

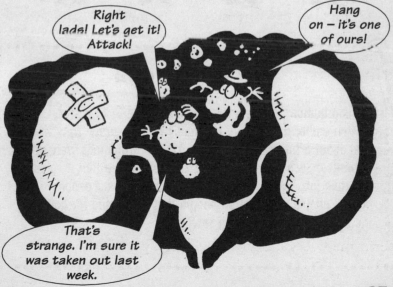

Can cloning cause problems? ....

Some people are scared of cloning because if scientists can clone a sheep, they could also clone humans. Dr Richard Seed made the headlines in January 1998 by saying that he was working on cloning a human being. He said that it 'was the first step to becoming one with God.' There will always be scientists who want to clone humans, and sooner or later, someone will succeed.

A Novel Idea

Cloning humans scares a lot of people because of a story written earlier this century by Aldous Huxley. *Brave New World* was about a future where different types of humans were grown in bottles. Each type had had its DNA altered so that it could do a certain job. There were leaders, superintelligent people, normal people, and mutant people that were used for doing all the nasty stuff like cleaning sewers.

If cloning humans becomes possible, people might want to clone dead relatives or famous popstars. They might even want to clone themselves so that they could live forever. Think about it – if a woman cloned herself and grew the new baby in her own womb, the baby would be the twin of its mother, not have a father, and be the daughter of her grandfather! Spooky!

One of the scariest things that might happen with human cloning is people growing whole copies of themselves. They might keep them in a storage shed and use them for spare parts!

So, cloning could be very useful to us, but it could also be very dangerous. We'll have to be very careful about what we do with it.

CHAPTER SEVEN

THE CRAZY HISTORY OF CLONING

You may think that it's only very recently that scientists have begun to clone animals. But believe it or not, they started to do it at the end of the 19th century. But because animal cells have the problem with shut-down DNA, they could only clone animal embryos. Animal embryos aren't as hard to clone as adult animals because none of the DNA in the embryo cells is shut down.

Animal Cloning Experiments, Part I
Switzerland, 1896

This is Hans Spemann.

He's very sick with a nasty lung disease called tuberculosis. He's had to go to a special hospital for the winter and he's not got much to do. He's forgotten to bring along any exciting novels to read, and PlayStations haven't been invented yet. The only book he's got is one about embryos. He decides to do an experiment.

Hans gets some fertilized eggs from a salamander — an amphibian like a frog.

Hans waits until the egg divides into two cells and then he separates the cells using a hair from his new-born baby son.

Each of the two separated cells grows into a new salamander. They are clones of each other.

Warning!
Do not read the next bit if you're squeamish.

Spemann tried to do his experiment again, but this time he didn't manage to split the two cells properly. A weird thing happened — the cells grew into a two-headed monster tadpole!

Be a Genetic Scientist:
CLONE A FROG!

If you are very patient and careful, you might be able to clone a frog at home. If you can't get this experiment to work, ask a science teacher at school to help you.

WHAT YOU'LL NEED

- some frog spawn from a pond
- water
- jam jars
- a shallow glass dish or plate
- a magnifying glass
- a very thin thread or hair

WHAT TO DO

1 Collect your frog spawn in the spring and bring it home in a jam jar full of pond water.

2 Get one or two frog spawn carefully out of the jar using a spoon and put them in some pond water into your dish. Stand the dish on white paper to make it easier to see what you're doing.

3 Keep checking the spawn, using your magnifying glass to help you see them properly.

When the spawn eggs have split into two cells, ask a friend to hold the magnifying glass for you. Then holding the hair carefully in both hands, lower it around and underneath the egg. Make sure the hair is in the middle of the egg, where the two cells are joined together. Pull your hands across so that the hair crosses over. Keep tightening the hair so that it cuts the two cells up.

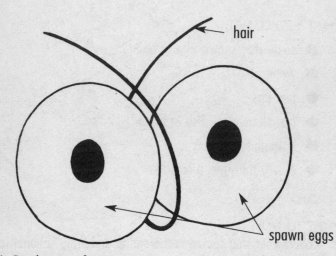

hair

spawn eggs

4 Do this to a few eggs.

5 Leave the cells to grow. Make sure there is enough pond water in the dish.

WHAT HAPPENS?
Sometimes, nothing will happen because the cells will die. They are delicate. But, if you're very careful, you will get two new tadpoles from one egg. Congratulations! You've cloned a frog embryo.

The next step... ....

Spemann thought that there might be a way of cloning an adult animal. He thought about growing a cell from an adult animal by putting it inside an egg.

Eggs are very special cells. They only have half the amount of DNA of other cells. Sperm also have only half the amount of DNA. When a sperm and egg join together, they have the full amount. The egg can only grow when it has this full amount of DNA.

It takes two, baby!

Ooh!

Spemann thought that if he took the nucleus out of an egg and put in the adult animal cell instead, the full amount of DNA from the animal cell would let the egg grow into an adult animal. Perhaps the DNA would not be shut off any more and the egg would grow?

But by the time someone did in fact manage to grow an animal by putting an adult cell inside an egg, Spemann had been dead for a long time.

Animal Cloning
Experiments Part II
USA, 1952

Here's a scientist called Robert Briggs. He took the nucleus out of a frog egg and then took a cell from a frog embryo. He put the cell into the egg and the egg grew into a tadpole!

So far, so good... ....

There was one big problem! Briggs and other scientists found out that tadpoles could hardly ever be cloned this way. And frog cells could not be cloned at all. Why? Because the cells had taken on a job and shut down some of their DNA.

Even though we couldn't clone frogs, scientists began to get excited about the idea of cloning humans.

If humans could clone themselves, we could control our own evolution! We could wait until people are 50 and then decide whether to clone them. Then we would get great thinkers, artists, athletes and beauties. A great person could spend his life from 55 onwards teaching his cloned children.

J B S Haldane, 1963

Cloning could allow us to fill the world with identical replicas of carefully chosen people.

Gunther Stendt, 1974

Cloning Millions

In 1978 in America, someone claimed to have helped a man actually clone himself!

A writer called David Rorvik said that a millionaire called Max had knocked on his door one day and asked him to find a doctor who could clone him. David had agreed to help. He found a doctor, the cloning was done on a secret island near Hawaii and a baby was born in 1976.

When scientists heard about this they were furious! Of course, it wasn't possible. But the book Rorvik wrote about this story became a bestseller and made him lots of money.

Scientists knew that the story about cloning a human couldn't be true. So far, they had only managed to clone a very young frog embryo, and even that had been tricky enough. Making a cloned mammal egg cell attach to the mother's womb is extremely difficult.

But in 1984, just as scientists were beginning to give up hope, Steen Willasden managed to clone a mammal embryo. He put nuclei from a sheep embryo into sheep eggs. Two lambs were born in 1984!

But we still couldn't clone an adult. The cells from the sheep embryo hadn't taken on a job and so none of their DNA had been shut down. To clone an adult animal, scientists would have to discover a way of making adult cells get all their DNA working. This is what the scientists at the Roslin Institute in Scotland managed to do. They took cells from an adult sheep, put them into sheep eggs, and in July 1996 Dolly was born!

But how did they do it? Let's find out by cloning a sheep ourselves!

CHAPTER EIGHT

TIME TO CLONE AN ADULT SHEEP

Right, are you ready? Then let's get cloning!

Step 1 ....

First of all, take some cells from a sheep. The cells used to make Dolly came from an udder. But you could take any cell from anywhere in the sheep. Apart from red blood cells, the only cells you can't use are eggs or sperm cells, because they have only half the DNA needed.

udder

Step 2 ....

Now make sure that the DNA in the cell is not switched off any more. There is a very simple and clever way of doing this. It involves something called the cell cycle.

The cell cycle

The cell cycle is a series of stages that a cell goes through when it is dividing into two new cells.

Straight after a cell has split into two, there is a time gap when each cell checks that it's got all its DNA. When it's sure that it has, it starts to grow.

Hmm, this seems fine. OK, you're clear to grow again!

When the cell has grown, it gets ready to divide again. Because each of the two cells will need a full set of DNA, the cell makes a complete copy of all its DNA.

Phew! That's all the copying done.

Then there is another gap, when the cell checks the DNA copy for any mistakes. Then the cell splits into two new cells.

But sometimes the cells have to rest. This usually happens when there isn't enough food for a cell to try to divide. The cells need food to give them enough energy to copy their DNA and split into two. If there isn't enough, they decide to stop dividing and have a little rest.

Now (this is the important bit) — when a cell is in the resting stage, all its DNA is switched on. This means that all the DNA in a resting cell can work!

But how can you make cells rest?

This is in fact very easy. You just don't give them any food. You starve them.

Cells in the laboratory are grown in a special liquid called cell culture liquid that has all the things they need to grow (like the jelly you grew your bacteria in). If you take most of the food out of the liquid, the cells stop dividing and rest. This saves their energy. It also means that none of their DNA is shut off any more!

Step 3 ....

So, now you have an adult cell with all the DNA working properly. You need an egg to put it into.

In sheep (as well as all other mammals), eggs grow in the ovaries. The ovaries have thousands of eggs in them, but they cannot all be fertilized. One egg at a time gets ready to be fertilised and is then sent out of the ovary down to the womb.

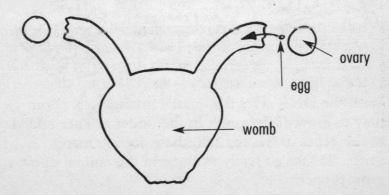

You can increase the number of eggs ready to be fertilised by giving your egg-donating sheep some hormones. The sheep can then be put to sleep and have the eggs removed in a simple operation.

Step 4 ....

You now have an egg whose nucleus has some DNA in it. It's only half as much DNA as a normal sheep cell, but you need to take this out.

Well, the DNA gives the animal instructions about how to grow. If the genes in the udder cell are added to the genes in the egg cell, there are too many genes. Things go really wrong and the animal doesn't grow properly.

How do I take the DNA out of the egg?

You have to use a microscope to see what you are doing because a sheep egg is much smaller than a frog egg. You hold the egg steady using a glass rod. Then you gently push a very narrow pipette (like a syringe) into the egg and ever so carefully suck out the nucleus. Easy!

Step 5

Now you've got an egg with no nucleus and a cell that you can clone.

Get the cell nucleus out the same way you've just got the egg nucleus out.

Put the cell nucleus into the egg.

Your clone is now ready to grow into a new sheep.

Step 6 ....

You need another female sheep to put your cloned egg
into, so that it can grow into a lamb. This sheep is
called a surrogate mother. It is useful if you use a
surrogate sheep that is a different colour to the sheep
that you're cloning. That way, you can prove that the
lamb is a clone.

Put the egg into the sheep using '*in vitro* fertilization'
or IVF. ('*In vitro*' is just a clever way of saying 'in a
test tube'. It means that you've fertilized an egg in a
test tube and you're now sticking the egg back into a
body. This technique is often used for human couples
who are finding it hard to have a baby.)

IVF is quite simple to do. Suck the egg up with a long syringe and then put the syringe into the sheep's vagina, go up through the womb, and into one of the fallopian tubes. Then squirt the egg out.

fallopian tube

The egg moves down the fallopian tube and back into the womb. By the time it gets there, it is ready to make a placenta, and can attach itself to the mother sheep. Then, all you have to do is sit back, have a cup of tea, and wait for your cloned sheep to be born. Congratulations!

CHAPTER NINE

THE FACE OF THE FUTURE

As you now know, cloning is a tricky, intricate procedure. Lots of things can go wrong with it. For instance, the egg is very tiny and easily damaged. Even the smallest syringe is very big compared to the egg. You have to be very careful about where you stick it, because a damaged egg will die!

Another problem with cloning is the IVF part. Getting the cloned eggs to attach themselves to the mother sheep is very difficult. It doesn't happen very often. To make Dolly, 277 eggs had to be used. Of the 277 eggs that had the nucleus from an udder cell put into them, only 13 developed into embryos. Those 13 were put into sheep, but only one managed to grow.

So, if you are going to clone sheep, you have to be very, very patient!

Where do we go from here? ....

In July 1998, scientists cloned
21 mice using the same
method that was
used to make
Dolly. This proved
that this way of
making clones really
works.

But, if we can now
clone any adult
animal, how far can we
go? Could we clone
ourselves? And what
about *Jurassic Park*, where
dinosaurs were cloned?
Could we bring back extinct species?

Can we clone ourselves?......................

The simple answer is yes! In fact, now we know how
to clone adult sheep and mice, we can clone any living
animal on Earth. Some countries are passing laws to
stop scientists cloning humans, because it is such a
terrifying thing to do. But because some scientists
might want to become famous, and might be paid an
awful amount of money for cloning, some people
think that it is only a matter of time before a human
clone is made.

Can we clone dinosaurs? ....

Probably not. And a good thing too if what happened in *Jurassic Park* is anything to go by! Who would want velociraptors roaming the streets?

In the film *Jurassic Park*, a scientist found mosquitoes in amber. These mosquitoes, like mosquitoes today, got their food by sucking blood out of animals. Imagine a little mosquito sucking the blood of a dinosaur. It goes to rest on a tree, but unknown to it, disaster is coming! The tree trunk is damaged and sap runs out. The sap engulfs the little mosquito and kills it!

When the tree sap hardens, it turns into a kind of rock called amber. Millions of years later, the amber is found, still with the fly perfectly preserved inside it. (If you see amber, it often has little flies inside.)

The idea in *Jurassic Park* was to take the blood out of the mosquito's stomach and find the dinosaur DNA in it. The DNA could be copied and put into an egg without its nucleus. The egg would grow into a new dinosaur.

This sounds like it would work, doesn't it? But there are lots of problems. Firstly, the amount of DNA you would get from the mosquito would be so small that it would be hard to do anything with it.

And even if you did get enough DNA, the mosquito could have sucked the blood of lots of dinosaurs. All the different dinosaur DNA would be mixed up. This could make a very strange dinosaur!

The main problem is that DNA can break down into lots of different bits. It can also be damaged. In the film, the bits of DNA were joined together with frog DNA to make up any missing bits. But we don't know how much DNA dinosaurs had! There could be a gene missing for something very important! And how on earth would we know which bits went where?

So, bringing back the dinosaurs doesn't look possible at the moment. But, cloning humans was thought to be impossible only a few years ago, so who knows what might happen in the future? Maybe you'll become a genetic engineer and show us!

Other OXFORD titles

Science Magic

Amazing books that reveal the secret science
behind some dazzling magic tricks!

Conjuring in the Kitchen:
ISBN 0–19–910520–0
Bewitched in the Bathroom:
ISBN 0–19–910521–9
Brainwaves in the Bedroom:
ISBN 0–19–910522–7
*Laboratory in the Living
Room:* ISBN
0–19–910523–5